Yesterday's Empire

Jay Wolfe

Published by Purple Unicorn Media

ISBN 978-1-910718-01-8

In Memoriam
Mum

YESTERDAY'S EMPIRE

Standing on the edge of yesterday's empire
A shattered realm and a lost facade
Slaughtered dreams drift through the night
Haunting ghost thoughts and icy shards
The morning dawning from the night before
The yearning calling to the past
The sweat soaked bed and bandaged head
Shifting hopes that never last.

Standing on the edge of yesterday's empire
Looking into the abyss
A shattered realm and a poisoned well
Cracked hope and it has come to this
A tattered standard
A battered shield
Ensigns frayed and hopes delayed
The temple walls defiled.

Standing on the edge of yesterday's empire
Nowhere to run and yesterday's sun
No longer shining
Yesterday's hope no longer dining
On the feasts of hope
All is gone, the world lies distraught
The walls fall down
The blasted town
The princess fled and was caught.

Standing on the edge of yesterday's empire
Nowhere to go
All the world's on fire
Shattered realms and battered homes
The walls are down
There's no one around
The blasted town
And all around
Lies deserted before the desert sun.

Standing on the edge of yesterday's empire
Standards torn lying in the mud
The horses slain, the world in rain
The Guard has flown, the gates are blown
The world lies open before the dawn.
Battered heart and a blasted start
The ruins smoulder in the fire
The dancers flee before the end
It would be their funeral pyre.

Standing on the edge of yesterday's empire
No more the dawn, the darkness lasts
The palace fired, from numerous blasts
We see the world in ruins lies.
Nowhere to go
All the world's afire
The gates are down
The enemy rides over the gate
The end is come
Is it too late?

Standing on the edge of yesterday's empire
Shattered realm and slaughtered dreams
Blasted hope, nothing's what it seems
The princess fled, she is not dead
A prison not a grave
The palace fell, we are not well
But still we can be saved.
The enemy rides, the gates are down
The horsemen canter into town
The world's in ruins, the world's afire
But our last remains
Just raises hope higher.

Standing on the edge of yesterday's empire
Will we fight or will we die
Imperial Guard it crests the hill
The Emperor drawn, hurt, unslain
The fight remains, the day still lasts
Accepting death is never as good as it seems.

Standing on the edge of yesterday's empire
Why should we die now
Why not fight, all through the night
Why not refuse
Why not resist
Why not insist
There can still be a way out of this

<u>OH, YESTERDAY</u>

Dangerous games in the Autumn sun
The leaves are orange, the sky is dun
Yesterday, oh yesterday
We ran the race
Oh....yesterday

Exploded bombs leave a hole of hate
The crater yearns, for the day it burns
The world turned round
We span around
Yesterday
Oh....yesterday

Shattered hearts and broken parts
The day we learned, the day that turned
The world that was, a pleasant place
Is now the darkness, lost without a trace
Yesterday, Yesterday
Oh...yesterday

THE DEAD CLAN

The Empire is Fallen
One of our keys is Gone
A young heart is Failing
The Sacred Clan is Ended

Scattered remnants
Broken hearts
Broken ensigns
Fallen realms

The dead clan lies prostrate
Devastation, disbelief
The old days, the calm days
Replaced with harsh new ways.

Ancient memes
Disastrous themes
A wipe out
A swipe out
Devastation
Resignation
Just defeat

POEMS OF A NONNY EWOLF

Dance alone
Or don't dance at all
Your only hope
Or your only dream
Usher in
What's new and fresh
A time to dance
No time to dream.
This world of ours
This sodden frame
Of desperate hope
Beside the stream.
Usher in
Intensive streams
Like a mountain goat
Dare to dance and dream
A time to sing
Sing a song of hope
No more the dark
Or a dim-light spark
We try to dream
Make a world of light
A world of hope
No more the dark.

I chase the light
To see it shine bright
Days of new dreams
Only what it seems
Each to their own
Shine a light on us
No more the dark
The dim-lit spark.
Have a new start
A day in the life
Vicarious spark
Each to their own vice.
The day dawns bright
Only shines the light
Bright shines the light
End times are in sight.
A dance of despair
Some days to care
No shadows cast bright
Only shines the light.
We can sink down
Make doom-laden groans
A testament
Not our testament.

A DUSK FILLED PAUSE

There's no way out now
Out now, out now
The door is fast
The lock is firm
The world is dark
The world has turned

Dance has turned to dust,
A dancing moment, a dusk filled pause
A moment lost
To the hopeless cause

We stagger on
The globe turns round
The ragged frond
Of a world unsound

DANCE WITH THE WOLVES

Dance with the wolves
On the final landing
Dance with the wolves
When life leaves you standing
Dance with the wolves
When you haven't a choice
Dance with the wolves

FLASH POEM

sapphire darts
piercing our hearts
dancing on the edge
abandoning the pledge
skirting the disaster
who knows what comes after
thrusting in the wind
We have always sinned
shining in the light
fighting through the night
Creating a new style
editing a file
Living a lie
Drinking the rye
And prancing, alighting
Punching and fighting
A way out of the night

<u>LANCERS</u>

lancers ride on a fiery night
sharp tipped points to impale
horse or man, lances do not care
they only dare

lancers push their mounts
they charge the lines
they roar and spur on to victory
or shattered bodies in defeat

lancers attack, lancers cry out
with banners billowing, hooves pounding
lancers charge the enemy
victory or death, all is one

EVE OF WAR

Watch the lamp posts
Is there anything new
Keep an eye on the lamp posts
And then you will know

EAMs fly across the ether
News blackouts suppress the truth
Diverting stories promoted by the media
D Notices served behind the scenes

Politicians bluster and fail to convince
Newspapers focus on the superficial
Blogs and tweets pass on the news
But few are listening, few believe

For war is coming, marching on the world
Watch the lamp posts, keep a keen eye out
The eve of war lies heavy on our soul
Enjoy the now for it will not last

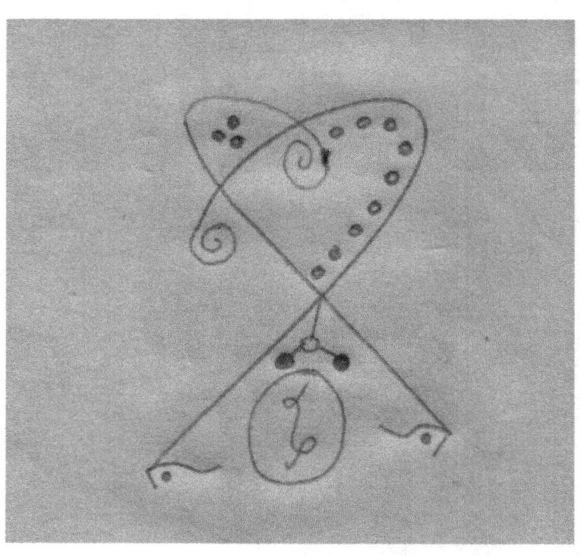

<u>LOVE POEM (1999)</u>

For a forgotten past
I name it
For a world no longer real
In these days when I proclaim it
Its gone
And only pain I feel

<u>END</u>

too many storms crash across the shore of my mind

devastating firestorms, dancing flames destroy the world

time preys ironic upon my latent hopes and screaming dreams

demons stalk the land, infernal fires sprouting from their hands

hope lies shrivelled, dauntless cries subdued to arrant whimpering

icons shattered and temples blasted as we seek tormented salvation

shipwrecks thrown up on the sands, time flown from many lands

dastards dance and dream and dreamers die and scream

negative commands evaporate under the streaming sun

the world lies screaming, dies a score of deaths

the banners shredded, the standard trampled unto dust

evil rides, the end is come

evil rides, and we are done

evil rides, and nothing can escape the dark

End Times

Dance the darkness
Because there's no other way

SUMMER DAYS

summer days
a misty haze
that lies upon
my memory

a dance, a song
a singalong,
the games we played
a moment strayed

summer time
so long ago
friends now lost
say it isn't so

oh summer days
through a misty haze
I remember you
do you remember me

<u>ONLY NOW</u>

mr wolf we have to move
maybe for the last time
one final dance
I hope not for the last time
but we have to take this chance
mr wolf
we have to move
we have to go
there is no no
we have to go
there is only now

<u>ONE DAY WE WILL GO</u>

one day we will go back again

but not until the curse is lift'd

I cannot run wild upon the beach

with folk with shotguns within easy reach

I cannot stand and mourn the day

when folk would kill me every way

THE SHADOWS CRY

the shadows cry out
don't forget us
don't forget us

parted souls
yesterday's empire
broken spirits
yesterday's laughter

the shadows cry
forlorn mournful shards
that cut into my heart

shattered souls
despairing spirits
cut from their hearts
too soon

the shadows
cry
why did we die

blasted lives
torn apart
before
their time

the shadows
cry

weep for us
remember us

the shadows
cry

<u>BUT</u>

But there wasn't
A way out of this
But there was not
A path to survive
But we died
and now we hide
But we lost
Oh sadness

WE LOST

<u>DREAMS OF ETERNITY</u>

dreams of eternity
wrecked by modernity
I don't know the next words
I've mislaid my goat herds
and all that I have got
is a sad depressed robot
just now

THE FINAL DAYS ARE OPENING FAST

The final days are opening fast
The times upon us will not last
The dawn of daylight in the leaves
And now its everyone who grieves

Darkness harrows our dim lit halls
Upon the deadly sea the siren calls
The end is nigh, the night is here
The world will end, the price is dear

Death tolls its harkened bell
Darkness breaks our hopeful spell
Nothing's left of the well dreamt realm
The ship's is rudderless, lost its helm

Nothing's left, we're all bereft
Feel the headman's axes' heft
Thank the stars we had our run
But now the darkness blocks the sun

The final days are here upon
The sweetness soured, the heart is gone
The missiles launched, we see their trail
If we live or die, we only fail

THERE'S NOTHING FOR ME

There's nothing for me
There's never anything of me
I'm a dead heart, dead beat
Dead meat, dead right
And my time lies begging
In the dark of night

Remove me from this equation
Delete me, cancel me out
Negate my existence.
I am a dark stain upon the multiverse
A shadow ripped upon life's wall
A darkness dwelt in once too often
A dread fear revealed

I am a shattered image
Dancing down the broken mirror
A warped chaos in the silver
A broken form disintegrating
Before my very eyes

<u>WE LOST</u>

we lost
we lost
we lost
...we lost

nothing grows
and nothing's left
we lost
we lost
we lost

empty words
and nothing's heard
we lost
we lost
we lost
... we lost

shattered hearts
of broken glass
we lost
we lost
we lost

desperate souls
crying in the wilderness
we lost
we lost

We Lost

<u>SHUT DOWN (FINAL DAY)</u>

come walk with me
down to the river
sit on the banks and cry
one last time

survival is over rated
when it is day by day tribulation
the world is a phantasm
some would say a cruel joke
but those who don't know humour

this is the end of me
this is the last day
the dying day
the final end
the only way

HALF MY DAYS

Half my days are bad days
Deep and down and dark
Most the rest are so-so days
Out and all around
But sometimes there's a good day
A day of rhyme and reason
But I always feel I borrow them
Days adrift from season

RABBITS RUN

Where have all my rabbits run
The burrow's bare and all have gone
The darkness spare, the dark is here
My rabbits run, my rabbits run

Standing on the edge of yesterday's empire

watching as the wreaths turn brown

And then the darkness of my life

Yesterday, oh yes-ter-day

I DON'T DO PEOPLE

I don't do people
They scare me
I don't live well within the world
Better lost within my mind
So sometimes I reach out
And burn myself
Sometimes I need to prove
That the world is harsh
By making it punish me
Sometimes I press where I should not
And receive the requisite kick
Sometimes I get lucky
And find the world exists
Tonight I am not so sure
Either way
Maybe the week will see
Maybe it will not

<u>A QUESTION OF EXISTENCE</u>

If you are bouncing off my weakness
To make a demand on others
Then you punish them for my sins
You fail

SHATTERED HOPES

Shattered hopes
Shattered dreams
Shattered world
Blasted screams

Broken hearts
Just
Broken hearts

DELTA FORCE

A life of nothing
A time of nothing
A zone of nothing
Nothing

The end time
The time when all dreams die
The time when forces coalesce
To constantly assail me

A dreadful void fills me now
Nothing is done
Nothing can be
Nothing remains

Hopeless pleasantries
Even these are attacked
Useless thanks and useless praise
Even these now wither

The end of everything
Of Life and dreams
And poetry
The end of words themselves

<u>THE DAY AFTER</u>

What day is it?
It's The Day After.
And tomorrow?
The Day After The Day After.
And after tomorrow?
The Day After that.

30th April 2014

In Memoriam of my Mum
Died yesterday

R.I.P.

MUM

Llyn Clywedog in the sun
Who was to know it would soon be done
The race of life would soon be run
No more laughter, no more fun

PASSED INTO GLORY TUESDAY 29TH APRIL 2014

www.purpleunicornmedia.com